The Art of Intercession:

The Tools of Prayer

Makiyah N. Jones

Copyright © 2023 Makiyah N. Jones

ISBN: 9798390839355

Scripture quotations marked AMP are taken from The Holy Bible, Amplified Bible ®. Amplified Version is a registered trademark of Crossway ®.

Scripture quotations marked GNT are taken from The Holy Bible, Good News Translation Version is a registered trademark of Crossway ®.

Scripture quotations marked MSG are taken from The Holy Bible, Message Version®. Message Version is a registered trademark of Crossway ®.

Scripture quotations marked NIV are taken from The Holy Bible, New International Version ®. New International Version is a registered trademark of Crossway ®

Scripture quotations marked NLT are taken from The Holy Bible, New Living Translation ®. New Living Translation is a registered trademark of Crossway ®

Dedication:

I would like to dedicate this book to all intercessors who aspire to grow deeper in the realm of intercession, and to those who are experiencing a barren season and need jolt. May you be reignited in prayer and may the fires of intercession blaze.

Acknowledgment:

I have carried the mantle for intercession within me for a long time, and now I feel like I have given birth to my baby! I was born for intercession! My journey with the Lord hinges on this foundation. I pray that this book will have an impact and that you will find the tools beneficial to your life of prayer.

I want to take a moment to acknowledge those intercessory teachers who played a pivotal role in my life. Thanks to Prophetess Tisha Black for her relentless place of intercession for kingdom, and her precision in discernment, which I observed firsthand. Thank you for affecting my life beyond measure. To my amazing, kind, grandmother Wyvonnie Jones, thank you for being an example of a house of prayer. You modeled intercession for me. Thank you for taking me to the altar every Friday night and teaching me how to cry aloud and spare not - "I AM" because of you.

I want to acknowledge some of the others who have had an impact on my journey as an intercessor over the years: Prophet Matthews, for your spirit of encouragement; Pastor Wylinda Brown for your courage and sacrifice; Prophetess Joan Styles for your perseverance; mother Marcia Daley, for her strength in prayer; Prophetess Kisha Cephus, for teaching me the skills of intercession, Prophetess Denise Ransom for her precision in intercession; Evangelist Carlina Wilkes for her dedication to intercession; Apostle Larraine McCaa for her relentless pursuit of God, Apostle Tonthalell Walters, for her warrior anointing. To my parents, Chrsitie and Henry Jones your act of obedience gave me life; thank you for loving and supporting always.

I also want to thank those forerunners who answered the call and birthed many moves of God in the earth which transcend time and space. The legacy of your seed lives on.

Table of Contents

Introduction:

The word of God is the one tool that every intercessor must learn to use effectively. Reading the word daily and meditating on the word is fundamentally important in stimulating your prayer life; it's the weight that builds your muscles of intercession. The word of God is the blueprint that navigates you in the place of intercession, thus it's vitally important to know the word. The Holy Spirit will highlight scriptures that speak directly to your personal life and will reveal the burden of intercession you may be carrying. Don't be hasty when reading the word but rather allow your entire being to become infused with the words you're reading. Be intentional about dissecting the word and give yourself over to its adventure.

Take time to hear what Heaven is releasing during your time of intercession. Your senses must be engaged because at any time the Holy Spirit will use them to communicate His intensions and bring revelation through the word. As you do this, Holy Spirit will provide you with an arsenal of powerful strategies during your time in intercession!

An intercessor stands in the gap for others. Intercessors are willing to stand between the person, people, nation etc. and their future. Intercessors identify and release the plans of Heaven for those whom they pray for, asking God's forgiveness and mercy on their behalf as if their sins were your own.

Intercession holds the potential of being one of the most exciting, inspiring, creative, and rewarding experiences one can have as a believer.

As an Intercessor, you are in partnership with God as He establishes His will in the earth through the vehicle of intercession, bringing freedom, salvation, healing and peace into regions, cities, nations, families, and individuals.

I have a question: Are you willing to pay the price of passionate prayer and intercession? Are you willing to make the necessary adjustments in your life to see God's Kingdom will and purpose done on earth as they are in Heaven? Are you willing to realign and adjust your priorities in life to be consumed by God's passion for His people and the world. In other words, do you truly desire the heart of the Father? Will you allow your heart to be broken with the things that break his heart? If your answer is yes, you are ready to take the journey with the

Holy Spirit.

As intercessors we must pray the word just as it is. We must be able to articulate exactly what Holy Spirit is revealing through His word. Speaking and praying the word of God aloud ministers to your spirit and feeds your soul. It allows your spirit to be edified as you read the word aloud. It is vital that an intercessor keep their spirit-man strong, healthy, aware, and vibrant.

Knowing the tools you need in intercession is important to every Intercessor. I've found in my journey as an intercessor that there are specific tools needed to maintain a committed and stable life of intercession. These tools have helped me along the way.

Many believers, even those in leadership, struggle at times with time management and constraints as it relates to intercession, however, of greater importance is our ability to recognize these moments and intentionally make time to commune with the Father in intercession. A lack of attention and purposeful drive will lead to a disconnect from your source, inevitably leading to prayerlessness and drought.

What is Prayer?

Prayer is interacting with God.

Isaac, Moses, Samuel, and Job all prayed, and their prayer yielded visible results which changed their lives for the better.

The first notable prayer was when Abraham pleaded with God not to destroy the people of Sodom.

Prayer is conversation with God in words or thoughts. Prayer can be a petition, thanksgiving, praise, adoration, and above all, it allows us to recognize that we are powerless in our lives apart from communion with our Maker and Redeemer.

Prayer is being in the moment, being present, and being open to spiritual realities. It is a way of learning to be ourselves. It is learning to abide in the presence of God, a presence that infuses every moment and space – but one to which we devote our attention to encounter the Divine.

In prayer you are dialoging with God. You address Him with adoration, confession, supplication, and thanksgiving.

Prayer is the womb by which the plans of God

are birthed in earth and deployed to advance the church, mankind, and our personal lives.

Prayer is a tool where the undiscoverable become discovered.

Prayer is interacting with God, most frequently through a spontaneous, individual, unorganized form of petitioning and/or thanking. *Praying* is a method of changing a situation for the better.

What is Intercession?

- o According to Oxford Dictionary, intercession is defined as the "action of intervening on behalf of another."

- o According to Cambridge English Dictionary, intercession is defined as "the act of using your influence to make someone in authority forgive someone else or save them from punishment."

- o According to Free Dictionary, intercession is "mediation in a dispute."

- o According to the International Standard Bible Encyclopedia, intercession had an original meaning, but the word's meaning has evolved from the Old Testament meaning to the New Testament meaning.

- o Intercession in the Old Testament was the word pagha`. Originally, it meant, "to strike upon," or "against." In a good sense, intercession meant "to assail anyone with petitions," or "to urge."

o Several scriptural examples show us that intercession is to the Lord but can also be made to people.

Tools That Help You Become More Skilled in Intercession:

1. Be Precise in Prayer!

o Avoid generalities in times of intercession. Remember you are standing in between that person, nation, region etc., thus your prayer must have precision. Be as clear and concise as possible during your time of intercession. This is targeted prayer - praying with a focus and the desired result in mind.

2. As intercessors we have two basic needs:

o To know God, His character, what He has done for us on the cross, and what we have inherited as a result.

o To know the enemy and his tactics.

3. Knowing what to pray for?

o The scripture gives us guidelines.

o The Holy Spirit will bring us the most urgent requests.

o We can ask, "Lord, how do you want me to pray for that person? Show me how to intercede." Remember that the Holy Spirit is our teacher, and He promises to help us (Romans 8:26, 27). He knows the mind of God and searches the deep things of the spirit and reveal them unto us.

o A vital point to remember is that when we pray, we have authority over the enemy, but not over the will of people.

4. Praying in the spirit

o Praying in the spirit is our spirit communicating directly with God (I Corinthians 14:2).

o Praying in the spirit is a perfect prayer. This means that when we pray in the spirit, the Holy Spirit (the Helper) intercedes through our spirit by praying a prayer that aligns with the perfect will of God (Romans 8:26-28).

o Praying in the spirit has definite meaning; although we don't understand what we are praying, God does.

o Praying in the spirit edifies the person praying. Praying in the spirit empowers us, builds us, strengthens us, and encourages us to continue with the Spiritual Warfare we are called to do (I Corinthians 14:4).

o Praying in the spirit has the authority of Heaven behind it. The Holy Spirit will prompt you at the opportune time (Ephesians 6:18).

5. Knowing Your Authority in Prayer

o The power of the Holy Spirit in us gives us authority to use the name of Jesus to stop the enemy.

o Scripture furnishes us clear guidelines on the authority Jesus promised us and which God has delegated to us.

  o "I have given you authority to trample on snakes and scorpions and to overcome all the power of the enemy" (Luke 10:19)

  o "That at the name of Jesus every knee should bow, in Heaven and on earth and under the earth" (Philippians 2:10).

o We can boldly pray this prayer: *"By the authority of Jesus and the precious blood of Jesus. I bind you Satan and break your powers over this situation. I loose (name) from your hold and destroy your works and assignment in Jesus' Name"*.

6. The Power of Agreement

o As intercessors, we agree with the Holy Spirit on that which He has called us to accomplish through spiritual warfare. We are called to be consistent with our prayers by the word of God and by the Spirit (Matthew 18:19-20). The Greek word for agree in this verse is *sumphoneo* which literally means "to sound together," to be harmonious.

o God doesn't call us to stand alone in our warfare against the enemy. It's in the prayer of agreement that we see greater results. Why? What is necessary for agreement in prayer? Why is the prayer of agreement so powerful?

o Acts 1:14: They all joined together constantly in prayer, along with the women and Mary the mother of Jesus, and with his brothers.

o Learning to pray in agreement is learning to pray in God's will.

o Also, if we are praying with another intercessor we must "agree to agree".

o Intercession starts in the heart of God (His idea, His initiative), then the Holy Spirit drops it into our heart, and we bring it back to God.

7. Fasting

o Jesus set an example, emphasizing that sometimes fasting is needed to rout out the enemy (Mark 9:29).

o Benefits: It brings victories where prayer alone cannot.

o Fasting should be viewed as a precious opportunity to get closer to the Lord.

o Revival is birthed through intense times of fasting and praying.

o Prayer and fasting brings the power of God in our lives. In history, God often led us to fast and pray for breakthroughs in our personal lives. Intercessors often experience much healing and breakthrough.
o Prayer and fasting bring wisdom, revelation, and guidance.
o Fasting chastens the body and teaches us self-control (1 Cor 9:27; 1 Cor.6:13-20).

8. **Word of God**

o If possible, have your Bible with you. God may want to give you direction or confirmation from it.
  o Psalm 119:105 – "Thy Word is a lamp to my feet and a light to my path."
o You can learn to use God's word against the plots of the enemy, just as Jesus did when tempted by him (Matthew 4).
o Take the helmet of salvation and the sword of the spirit, which is the Word of God (Ephesians 6:17).
o The Word of God creates. The Word of God cannot return void (Isaiah 55:11).
o We don't have to spend a lot of time wrestling with the enemy. We pray from a place of dominion in the spirit.
o Praying the word of God holds God accountable for what he has said and the

promises he has made towards us. God is not a man that he should lie nor the son of man that he shall repent.

9. <u>Faith</u>

o When entering intercession your faith must be strong. Praying without faith will not yield results in prayer.
o Faith requires you to work the word of God in your time of Intercession.
o For as the body without the spirit is dead, so faith without works is dead also." (James 2:26)
o In obedience and faith, utter what God brings to your mind, believing.
  o John 10:27 – "My sheep hear My voice, and they follow Me.
o Keep asking God for direction, expecting Him to give it to you. He will.
  o Psalm 32:8 – "I will instruct you and teach you the way you should go; I will counsel you with my eye upon you."
o Embrace faith and God's grace to confront what would seem to be insurmountable obstacles.
  o Matthew 17:20- He replied, "Because you have so little faith. I tell you the truth, if you have faith as small as a mustard seed, you can say to this

mountain, 'Move from here to there' and it will move. Nothing will be impossible for you.

- o Prophesy with faith and confidence that which we know to be God's will over lives and situations.
  - o Ezekiel 37:4-5- *4* "Then he said to me, "Prophesy to these bones and say to them, 'Dry bones, hear the word of the Lord! *5* This is what the Sovereign Lord says to these bones: I will make breath enter you, and you will come to life. Jesus did this at the grave of Lazarus:
  - o John 11:41-43– *41* "So they took away the stone. Then Jesus looked up and said, "Father, I thank you that you have heard me. *42* I know that you always hear me, but I said this for the benefit of the people standing here, that they may believe that you sent me." *43* When he had said this, Jesus called in a loud voice, "Lazarus, come out!"

Helpful Tools When Engaging in

Intercession:

- o We must have an attitude of adoration, reverence, praise, and HONOR.

- o We must avail ourselves in a spirit of submission to His ways and will. (REPENTANCE IS REQUIRED)

- o We must acknowledge our dependence on him to supply our need by asking for sustaining substances naturally and spiritually.

- o Approach Him in the spirit of forgiveness towards others as we petition for pardon from him.

- o UNFORGIVENESS IS A HINDRANCE TO ANSWERED PRAYERS (Matthews 6:14-15)

- o Acknowledge the Fathers Sovereignty.

- o Make very sure your heart is clean before God by giving the Holy Spirit time to convict in case there is any unconfessed sin. (Psalm 66:18)

- o Acknowledge that you cannot pray without the Holy Spirit. (Romans 8:26) o Die to your own imaginations, desires, and burdens for how you think you should pray. (Proverbs 3:5-6; Proverbs 28:26)

o Ask God to bear positive witness with you by the Holy Spirit, and then thank Him in faith for doing so. (Ephesians 5:20)

o Praise God in faith for the remarkable prayer time you are going to have. He is a remarkable God and will be consistent in His character.

o Deal with the enemy from a place of dominion. Come against him with boldness & authority and with the sword of the Spirit. (James 4:7)

o Wait in silent expectancy. Then in obedience and faith, speak only what God speaks to you, believing His Word, "My sheep hear My voice." Don't move to the next subject until God is through with that one.

o Always take a moment to listen after prayer: God is always speaking.

o Remember: intercession is communication.

o Always have your Bible with you or near you just in case God wants to give you a scripture for confirmation and /or direction. (Psalm 119:105) o When God is done speaking, praise Him for what He is doing and what He has spoken during your time of intercession. Remind yourself that "to God alone is the glory." (Romans 11:36)

o As you prepare to pray, quiet your heart and mind by reading scriptures. Do not presume that a request is not worthy. Only God knows the complete situation. Your obedience to pray is the vehicle through which God's love will flow.

o After you have prayed, release your prayers to God. Do not try to carry the burdens on your own shoulders, and do not let the petitions drag you down, either spiritually or emotionally.

o Sometimes our intercessors experience "dry periods" or times when we feel far from God.

o Here are four things that you can do during these times:

  o Wait patiently upon the Lord.
  o Continue to read your word.
  o Sing, read or listen to favorite worship songs, artist, and instrumentals.
  o And above all...keep praying.

o Remember the promises of the Lord toward you: "You did not choose Me, but I chose you and appointed you that you should go and bear fruit, and that your fruit should remain, that whatever you ask the Father in My name He may give you" (John 15:16)

When going into Intercession remember the following tools:

1. Maintain a strong personal prayer life - Matthew 6
2. Wait on the Lord and posture yourself in faith - Isaiah 40
3. Sense the prophetic anointing and stir yourself.
4. Agree with others and pray in unity.
5. Flow with the Holy Spirit - intercession is initiated by the Holy Spirit.
6. Pray in the Spirit - begin in the faith.
7. Pray the scriptures.

How To Enter Prayer:

- Thanksgiving: (Psalm 100:4) Thankfulness is the surest way to direct your attention toward the Lord and make a heart connection with Him in which you can sense the lines of communication are open.

- Adoration: Reminding God of who he is, I worship you, my God, because of who you are: (You are great, you are mighty, you are perfect in all your ways, you are God, etc.)

- Reverence: (John 14:15) God wants a relationship, to be a Father and to commune with us. We must know that God is holy, mighty, and worthy to be reverenced.

- Forgiveness: Asking God Forgiveness of your sins both known and unknown. This allows you to enter prayer with a clean heart.

- Repentance: Begin to repent of those things you have done throughout the day that does not align to the will, purpose, or plan of God. Repent for both knowing and unknowing sins.

- Confession: Confession cleanses us and allow us to grow in our prayer life, in our life with Christ and in our Spiritual Life and be conformed in the image of Christ. Unconfessed sin can block us from the presence of the Lord, (Ps. 139:23-24)

o Focus: Focus on you and God limit all distractions

o Honest- When entering prayer, you must be honest. Be transparent and clean before the Lord, desiring truth in the innermost parts of your life.

o Have an Open Heart: Open your heart and let Him in. Know that you can come to Him with an honest heart because He sees you and knows everything about you and still loves you.

o Boldness- Hebrews 4:16

o Separate Yourself: There is a place in prayer where God meets you, but it's not a building. It's not even your body. It's a place in God which is in the Spirit. God has prepared a place in Him just for you.

o Believe: Have faith in God's power to do what He has promised and remember that you pray he answers. (Mark 9:24)

o Matthew 15:8 - Remember it's important that when entering prayer that you don't just offer lip service but that our heart must be properly postured before the Father.

God's Reason for Prayer &

Intercession:

o Prayer is more than just asking God to meet our needs; prayer is God's plan for us to know Him better and establish a relationship with him.

o Prayer isn't about what we can get out of God and what God can do for us, but God revealing to us who he is to us.

o Prayer is the way in which we learn to communicate with God and hear His voice.

o Prayer is important because it allows us to abide (live) in Him and allow Him to live through us. (John 15:4)

o Prayer is important because it allows us to be purified in him.

o One of the greatest secrets of prayer is to align ourselves to God's purposes rather than seeking to align God to ours (we can forget it; we can never align God to our way). (Remember when we pray, we must pray according to his will, his purpose, and his plan.)

o Until we totally gain an understanding of the importance of prayer and having a lifestyle of prayer, we will remain in cycles and remain in stagnation. PRAY MUST BE A LIFESTYLE, PRAYER IS A LIFESTYLE, you can't choose when you want to prayer. You can't just pray in hard times, but you must keep a consistent lifestyle of prayer.

o "The plans of the LORD stand firm forever, the purposes of his heart through all generations" (Ps.33:11)

Finale: Things to Remember When Praying

o We must understand: God's Will (Praying according to the will of God), We must understand God's Plan, and we must Understand God's Purpose.

Understanding God's will:

o We must Trust in the Lord with all our hearts and lean not unto our own understanding but in all our ways we acknowledge Him and He will direct our path (Proverbs 3:5); and we pray one for another.

o We come boldly before the throne of grace, that we may find grace to help in the time of need (Hebrews 4:16).

- o We cast all our cares upon Him for He cares for you; and give thanks in all things (1 Peter 5:7).

Prayer in Action:

Revelation comes through prayer.

Fellowship and communion with the Father through the Holy Spirit release His power to pray effectively to produce fruit – to heal the sick, cast out devils and raise the dead.

John 15:7-8 (AMP) - "If you live in me (abide really united to Me) and My words remain in you and continue to live in your hearts, ask whatever you will, and it shall be done for you. When you bear (produce) much fruit, My Father is honored and glorified, and you show and prove yourselves to be true followers of Mine."

Christ has planned for you to bear much fruit! When God's power flows through you to bring healing and deliverance to the world, it brings glory to Him! The key to asking in prayer and receiving whatever you ask lies in your relationship with and in knowing He called you and anointing you for this position. (John 15:16). This is prayer in action.

When we look at prayer in action, I often think of the story of Elijah in the book of 1 Kings. Elijah was a prophet, a mighty man of God, whose prayers superseded the laws of nature. Through his prayers God revealed Himself as the all-powerful one and only true living God. Elijah prayed and the Heavens were shut so that it did not rain for three and a half years. His prayer was not a long-drawn-out prayer, it was prayer in action, and it was also a bold, daring prophetic declaration that God directed him to make publicly before King Ahab. God did this in 4 Steps. This strategy will give you insight on the tools needed.

The Strategy of Prayer in that was demonstrated by Elijah:

1. **Hear** the Word of the Lord - I Kings 17:1 *"As the Lord God of Israel lives, before whom I stand, there shall not be dew nor rain these years, but according to my word."* Elijah was not speaking in his own authority. His words were divinely anointed, directed and empowered by God.

2. **Believe** the Word of the Lord - At the appointed time God spoke to Elijah, I Kings 18:1 *"Go, show thyself unto Ahab; and I will send rain upon the earth."* It was time for a divine confrontation! He had his assignment and he obeyed.

3. **Speak** the Word of the Lord - There was a secret power behind Elijah's prayers. Elijah's **faith** and **confidence** were neither in himself nor his abilities he possessed. His unshakeable faith and total dependence were on God Almighty! He had an intimate relationship with God, and he knew God would do exactly what He had spoken. I Kings 18:36,37 *"Lord God of Abraham, Isaac, and of Israel, let it be known this day that thou art God in Israel, and that I am thy servant, and that I have done all these things at thy Word. Hear me, O Lord, hear me, that this people may know that thou art the Lord God, and that thou hast turned their heart back again."*

4. **Expect** the Supernatural – Immediately God answered by fire! God's glory and power were manifested. When the people saw the fire, they fell prostrate on their faces and cried out, *"The Lord, He is God! The Lord, He is God!"* - I Kings 18:39, NIV

Here are a few things you should remember and save in the archives of your heart when you are putting prayer in action. Each of these has been essential to my life as an intercessor. I have seen them work I am living in the manifestation thereof.

It's always good to pray and when you pray you must have an action plan therein lies answered prayers.

Things to remember:

- Prayer is one of the greatest, essential tools to use on earth to deploy the plans of God and advance the church, mankind, and your personal life.
- Prayer is the lifeline in which God's power moves.
- An individual is only as strong, in the spirit, as their prayer life.
- Prayer is a tool used to defeat the plans of the enemy.
- Prayer is a tool used to dismember and destroy the weaponry of the enemy.
- Prayer is a tool used to launch the mysteries of Heaven.
- Prayer is a tool used to discover treasures on the inside of you.
- Prayer is a tool used to discover ancient mantles that were left undiscovered.
- Prayer is the tool that reveals the plot, snares, twist, and entanglements of the enemy.
- Prayer is the tool where the undiscoverable becomes discovered.
- Prayer is a tool used to strike confusion in the camp of the enemy.
- Prayer is a skill of proficiency needed by all mankind.

o Prayer releases the hidden secrets in the chambers of God's heart.

o When you pray, you must pray from a pure heart. When entering the chambers of prayer, your heart must be properly postured. We must ask, as David did, in psalms 51:10 dash ask the Lord to creating us a clean heart.

> o Psalm 51:10 – "Create in me a clean heart, O god and renew a right spirit within me."

o Praying in the wrong spirit will yield no fruit, but it will produce cycles of frustration. It is important as intercessors that when praying we pray in the right spirit.

o Prayer is a tool of authority. When you pray you have the power to overturn policies, laws, and agendas warranted by hell.

o intercessors are people of power who must walk in authority.

o Prayer has the power to reroute the destination of those in the earth realm.

o The prayers of many believers have the power over the affairs of the world.

o The Bible states in Matthew 18:20 that where two or three are gathered in my name I am there in the midst. Prayer, in unity, has the power to destroy and overrule demonic security councils.

The Sound of an Intercessor:

Romans 8:26 (NLT) - And the Holy spirit helps us in our weaknesses. For example, we do not know what God wants us to pray for. But the Holy Spirit prays for us with groanings that cannot be expressed in words.

o Intercessors have the power to change lives, families, cities, states, nations, and continents.
o When intercessors pray, mankind must yield to the sound of the intercessor. Intercessors carries frequencies, that penetrate and shift the vibration of mankind.
o Intercessors don't faint, but they pressed through and prayer.
o There is strength and prayer.
o There are answers in prayer.
o There are visions in prayer.
o There are keys released in prayer.
o There are strategies released in prayer.
o There is healing through prayer.
o There is breakthrough in prayer.
o There is hope in prayer.
o There are answers to unanswered questions in prayer.

- Prayer is a substance in which we must daily partake of to live a life of complete sanity and serenity.
- Prayer should be a priority in every person's life.
- Prayer is a tool that keeps the oxygen of God flowing through the body of mankind.
- prayer is the foundation of the earth.
- Prayer is a birthing ground.
- Prayer can shift and change the character of individuals.
- The church is unified by prayer.
- There is a sound in prayer to shift the entire anatomy of the earth realm.
- Prayer has a sound that will shift the entire world of economics.

There Are Many Ways To Pray:

OPEN YOURSELF TO GOD: As you begin your time of prayer, find a quiet space, turn off your phone, the television and any other distractions that may keep you from fully entering this time of prayer. Take several deep breaths to quiet your mind and heart and spend some moments in quiet awareness in the presence of Jesus. Invite the Holy Spirit to guide you as you reflect on God's Word.

Prayer is communication between you and God, the Father.

o You can pray by having a normal conversation.
o You can pray through singing.
o You can pray through art.
o You can pray through creativity.
o You can pray through sound (the sound of minstrels).
o You can pray silently.
o You can pray aloud.
o You can pray by shouting out.
o Your tears are slash can be prayers.
o You can pray with the extension of your hands.
o You can pace back and forward in prayer.
o You can lay prostrate on the floor to pray.

o You can kneel down to pray you can take moments
   to go on walks and pray.

When engaging in prayer at the end of the day.
Here are a few tools that will help you.

1. Place yourself in God's presence. Give thanks for
   God's great love for you.
2. Pray for the grace to understand how God is
   moving in your life.
3. Thank God for His goodness toward you.
4. Review your day — recall specific moments and
   your feelings at the time.
5. Reflect on what you did, said, or thought in those
   instances. Were you drawing closer to God, or
   further away? Give thanks for that which drew
   you closer and ask for forgiveness in areas in
   which you fell short.
6. Look toward tomorrow — think of how you might
   collaborate more effectively with God's plan. Be
   specific. Conclude with a prayer.

Why Do We Prioritize Prayer?

Luke 18:1 (AMP) – *"Now Jesus was telling the disciples a parable to make the point that at all times they ought to pray and not give up and lose heart."*

- We are commanded to pray.

  o ***1 Chronicles 16:11 (NLT)*** – *"Search for the Lord and for his strength; continually seek him."*

  o ***Matthew 7:7 (MSG)*** - *"Don't bargain with God. Be direct. Ask for what you need. This isn't a cat-and-mouse, hide-and-seek game we're in."*

  o ***Ephesians 6:18 (ESV)*** - *"...praying at all times in the Spirit, with all prayer and supplication. To that end, keep alert with all perseverance, making supplication for all saints."*

  o ***Matthew 6:6 (ESV)*** – *"But when you pray, go into your room and shut the door and pray to your Father who is in secret. And your Father who sees in secret will reward you."*

- Jesus is the model for prayer.

  o *Mark 1:35 (ESV)* – *"And rising very early in the morning, while it was still dark, he departed and went out to a desolate place, and there he prayed."*

  o *Mark 6:46 (NIV)* - *"After leaving them, he went up on a mountainside to pray."*

  o *Luke 5:16 (NIV)* – *"But Jesus often withdrew to lonely places and prayed."*

  o *Luke 6:12 (NIV)* – *"One of those days Jesus went out to a mountainside to pray and spent the night praying to God."*

  o *Hebrews 5:7 (GNT)* – *"In his life on earth Jesus made his prayers and requests with loud cries and tears to God, who could save him from death. Because he was humble and devoted, God heard him."*

Taking time away to pray:

It is important to take moments away from everything and everyone to commune with the Lord. Jesus showed us an example of this in Matthew 14:23 when He sent the multitudes away and went up into a mountain, alone, to pray.

Exercise and commit to a time of prayer and meditation with the Lord. Journal and record what God speaks to you.

- You can take 15 minutes of prayer alone.

- You can take 30 minutes of prayer alone.

- You can take 4 hours of prayer and meditation.

- You can take 12 hours of prayer and meditation.

- You can take 24 hours of prayer and meditation alone.

What times are you committing to pray?

Morning

_____

_____

_____

Afternoon

_____

_____

_____

Evening

_____

_____

_____

Night

_____

_____

_____

5 Days of Journaling:

Your Experience in Prayer

Day 1

_____

_____

_____

_____

_____

_____

_____

_____

_____

_____

_____

_____

_____

_____

_____

_____

_____

_____

_____

_____

_____

_____

_____

_____

_____

_____

_____

Day 2

Day 3

_____

_____

_____

_____

_____

_____

_____

_____

_____

_____

_____

_____

_____

_____

_____

_____

Day 4

_____

_____

_____

_____

_____

_____

_____

_____

_____

_____

_____

_____

_____

_____

_____

_____

_____

_____

Day 5

_____

_____

_____

_____

_____

_____

_____

_____

_____

_____

_____

_____

_____

_____

_____

_____

When To Pray:

We are to always pray. The Bible says in Luke 18:1 that man ought to always pray and not lose heart.

Intercessors are to pray:

o   When you gain burdens for prayer.
o   When there is no burden.
o   When you feel like praying.
o   When you don't feel like praying.
o   When someone weighs heavy on your heart.
o   When you think of someone constantly.
o   When everything inside of you resists praying.
o   When you feel like giving up on God.
o   When you are happy.
o   When you are sad.
o   When you are frustrated.
o   When it seems like everything is going wrong.
o   When you have completed goals.
o   When you are successful.
o   When you feel like you have failed.
o   When you are discouraged.
o   When you are weary.
o   When you are encouraged.
o   When you feel alone.
o   When you doubt yourself.

o When you feel overwhelmed.

o When you feel hopeless.

o When you receive answers to prayer.

o When you are tired.

o When you are fasting.

o When you are not fasting.

Indications that God is prompting you to intercede:

1. You feel a burden for other people.
2. You feel led to pray for someone.
3. You have sudden urges to pray in the Spirit.
4. You are sensitive and prone to mood swings that affect your spirit.
5. You find yourself saddened, grieving, or weeping at unusual times and places.
6. You experience an overwhelming sense of heaviness.
7. You find yourself being easily agitated or overly sensitive.
8. You awaken at odd hours of the night for no obvious reason.
9. You have repeating descriptive dreams which you can remember.
10. You discern the significance and symbolism of circumstances.
11. You have a desire to pray more, but often don't

know how or what to pray.

12. You read a book, go to a seminar, or hear someone speak on intercession and it stirs your spirit.

It is important to have set times to pray and spontaneous times to pray also. David said in Psalm 55:17 "evening and morning and a non will I pray and cry aloud and he shall hear my voice."

Here are times you can pray:

o Pray in the morning when you wake up and when you are leaving home.
o In the afternoon.
o In the evening.
o In the night.
o Before you go to sleep at night.
o Throughout the night.

Length of Prayer:

There is no specified prayer time frame that you must pray. You don't always have to pray long. Sometimes prayers can be three to five words.

o You can pray one sentence.
o You can pray long prayers.
o You can pray short prayers.

Ways to pray with the help of the Spirit:

There are many ways to pray.

Romans 8:26 - "In the same way, the Spirit helps us in our weakness. We do not know what we ought to pray for, but the Spirit himself intercedes for us through wordless groans."

o Your tears are a language in prayer.
o Your sighs are a prayer language.
o Your groans are a prayer language.
o You can pray with known tongues.
o You can pray with unknown tongues.
o Your silence, in His presence, can be a prayer language.

What Happens Through Prayer:

It is important to make prayer an occupation. Through prayer you can:

o Satisfy God's heart.
o Overthrow the agenda of Hell.
o Regain the lost.
o Regain lost territory.
o Gain momentum for forward movement.
o Through prayer visions are manifested.
o Through prayer purpose is revealed.
o Through prayer we receive empowerment.
o Through prayer we are able to fulfill the will of God.
o Through prayer purpose is revealed.
o Through prayer we are able to discover Heaven's solutions for the earth.
o Through prayer we gain safety.
o Through prayer God gives us the ability to experience His glory.
o Through prayer we are able to prevail over evil
o Through prayer we are refocused.
o Through prayer anxiety is eliminated in your life.
o Prayer releases healing. (When Abraham prayed there was healing released
o Victory starts with prayer.
o Through prayer you can achieve authority and

dominion. (Genesis 1:26)
o Prayer brings your life into divine alignment.
o Prayer helps you overcome the greatest attacks in life.
o Prayer is Heaven's process that prepares you for promotion both naturally and spiritually.
o Prayer takes you into new places.
o You can overcome the evil one through prayer. (Remember evil comes in many ways lack, fear, poverty, and many more.)
o You must learn how to resist the enemy through prayer.
   o James 4:7 (NIV) – "Submit yourselves, then, to God. Resist the devil, and he will flee from you."

o We find our identity in prayer (2 Peter 1:2-4). When you learn how to pray God shows you your true identity.
o Prayer is not an activity but a responsibility (2 Chronicles 7:14, 1 Peter 2:1).
o Prayer is a spiritual law, and it guarantees specific outcome, and it works for everybody everywhere (Luke 18:1-8).
o We must understand when we pray God is going to answers us.
o Prayer is preparation for what's to come.
o Prayer unlocks promises.
o Prayer unlocks blessings.
o Prayer is your place of protection (Psalms 91:1).

o Prayer brings forth change.

It is important for intercessors to maintain a prayer life. Without a prayer life, you become prayerless and disconnects set in. Where prayerlessness exits there is a reduction of the time spent in prayer. As intercessors you must continue to invite the spirit of prayer into your life.

Why Intercessors Are Necessary:

- There is a shortage of intercessors in the land which highlights the necessity of intercessors.
- Without intercessors, the entire earth realm remains stagnant.
- When intercessors move away from their posts, calamity befalls the land.
  - 2 Chronicles 7:14 informs us why intercessors are necessary.
- Without intercessors, the Heavens will remain closed.
- Intercessors are necessary because they stand before the courts of Heaven and plead the cases of men in land.
- God searched for intercessors in Ezekiel 22:30 to stand in the gap and make up the hedge.
  - Are you the kind of intercessor God is searching for?
- Intercessors have the power to change situations.
  - Are you the kind intercessor God is searching for?

Prayer Builds Stamina

- Stamina means the ability to sustain prolonged physical or mental effort.

o Stamina is needed in the life of individuals. It gives one the ability to endure and persevere. Without prayer your life will be devoid of divine direction for your life and destiny.

o Prayer broadens your range in the spirit.

o There are several dimensions of prayer.

The Strategy to Prayer

o Strategic intercession should focus primarily on issues revealed by the Holy Spirit as it relates to a people, community, local church, city, nation and world. The intercessor should maintain their focus on the bigger picture and priorities, especially when praying together with others.

o Without prayer, nothing is solidified in the spirit.

o Intercessors create pathways.

o Prayer ignites revival.

o Prayer is the foundation for revival.

o Prayer reveals destiny.

o Prayer opens the scroll of your life.

o Prayer unlocks scrolls.

o Prayer is rewarding.

o Prayer is a lifestyle.

Five Causes of a Poor Prayer Life:

What causes one's prayer life to become stagnant or experience season of drought and death, or even seasons of elevation and decline. In this chapter we will explore some of the pitfalls that lead to the ruin of one life of prayer.

1. Some would attribute their poor prayer life to disappointments. They prayed but did not seem to get a favorable answer from the Lord. This is due to a wrong attitude to prayer – an attitude that is self-centered rather than God-centered. *"Ye ask, and receive not, because ye ask amiss, that ye may consume it upon your lusts."* (James 4:3).

2. Some may blame their lack of prayer on their busy schedule. They can hardly find time to pray because of their many commitments at work, school, or home. This is due to an unbalanced order of priorities. As greater priority is given to other pursuits and concerns in life, prayer is gradually pushed down the list to a lower level of priority.

3. Some find it difficult to pray because of wandering thoughts. This is due largely to a

lack of self-discipline and insufficient preparation of heart (Job 11:13).

4. Some are not able to pray well because of ongoing relationship problems. According to 1 Peter 3:7, a husband's prayers may be hindered if he is not dwelling with his wife according to knowledge and giving her the honor that is due to her.

5. Some experience seasons of spiritual dryness when they have little desire to pray. This is often due to disobedience or unconfessed sins. *"When I kept silence, my bones waxed old through my roaring all day long. For day and night thy hand was heavy upon me: my moisture is turned into the drought of summer."* (Psalm 32:3-4).

Preventing a Poor Prayer Life:

1. Make your prayers God-centered. Seek the accomplishment of God's will, not your own. *"After this manner therefore pray ye: Our Father which art in Heaven, hallowed be thy name. Thy kingdom come. Thy will be done in earth, as it is in Heaven."* (Matthew 6:9-10, cf. 26:42).

2. Assign a high priority to prayer. *"Praying always with all prayer and supplication in the Spirit and watching thereunto with all perseverance and supplication for all saints."* (Ephesians 6:18). Martin Luther once said that the busier he got, the more time he would spend in prayer. When something is important to you, you will always make time for it. The same principle applies to prayer.

3. Be disciplined when you pray. *"Watch and pray, that ye enter not into temptation: the spirit indeed is willing, but the flesh is weak."* (Matthew 26:41, cf. 1 Peter 4:7). Remove all distractions and interruptions (e.g., Turn off your handphone). Do not rush into prayer. Spend a few moments to calm your

mind and to *"be still and know that I am God."* (Psalm **46:10**).

4. Always be sure that you mean whatever you say in prayer. Do not just mouth the words and use the same stock phrases over and over again in your praying. *"This people draweth nigh unto me with their mouth, and honoureth me with their lips; but their heart is far from me."* (Matthew **15:8**). Think carefully about everything that you say to God. *"Be not rash with thy mouth and let not thine heart be hasty to utter anything before God: for God is in Heaven, and thou upon earth: therefore, let thy words be few."* (Ecclesiastes **5:2**).

5. Settle any relationship problems that may be hindering your prayer life. *"Therefore, if thou bring thy gift to the altar, and there rememberest that thy brother hath ought against thee; Leave there thy gift before the altar and go thy way; first be reconciled to thy brother, and then come and offer thy gift."* (Matthew **5:23-24**). Do not harbor a bitter or unforgiving spirit against anyone.

6. Confess your sins regularly. Do not allow them to accumulate and "clog up" your channel of communication with God. *"Blessed is he whose transgression is forgiven, whose sin is*

covered...I acknowledged my sin unto thee, and mine iniquity have I not hid. I said, I will confess my transgressions unto the LORD; and thou forgavest the iniquity of my sin." (Psalm 32:1-5)

7. Cultivate a thankful spirit toward God. There are so many blessings that we tend to take for granted: Health, well-being, safety, family, peace and stability. *"In everything give thanks: for this is the will of God in Christ Jesus concerning you."* (1 Thessalonians 5:18)

8. Meditate on Bible verses on prayer. E.g., Jeremiah 33:3 – *"Call unto me, and I will answer thee, and shew thee great and mighty things, which thou knowest not";* James 5:16 – *"Confess your faults one to another, and pray one for another, that ye may be healed. The effectual fervent prayer of a righteous man availeth much."* Write them down and place them in prominent places where you can see them and be reminded to pray.

9. Keep a prayer journal or diary. Record whatever you prayed for and how it was answered. E.g. *"I cried by reason of mine affliction unto the LORD, and he heard me; out of the belly of hell cried I, and thou heardest my voice."* (Jonah 2:2) Review it from time to time.

Many of the psalms are recorded prayers.

10.   Keep company with brethren who pray. The more you associate closely with prayerful people, the more you will want to pray. *"And it came to pass, that, as he was praying in a certain place, when he ceased, one of his disciples said unto him, Lord, teach us to pray, as John also taught his disciples."* (Luke 11:1).

What Hinders Your Life of Prayer Intercession?

What hinders me in Intercession?

Ye ask and receive not because ye ask amiss, that ye may consume it upon your lusts. (James 4:3)

- o If you want to pray and intercede properly you must identify hindrances to effective intercession and eliminate these from your life. A "hindrance" is anything that stands in your way, preventing you from interceding.

- o Sin of any kind: Isaiah 59:1-2; Psalm 66:18; Isaiah 1:15; Proverbs 28:9

- o Idols in the heart: Ezekiel 14:1-3

- o An unforgiving spirit: Mark 11:25; Matthew 5:23

- o Selfishness, wrong motives: Proverbs 21:13; James 4:3

- o Power hungry, manipulative prayers: James 4:2-3

- o Wrong treatment of marriage partner: I Peter 3:7

o Self-righteousness: Luke 18:10-14

o Unbelief: James 1:6-7

o Not abiding in Christ and His Word: John 15:7

o Lack of compassion: Proverbs 21:13

o Hypocrisy, pride, meaningless repetition: Matthew 6:5; Job 35:12-13

o Not asking according to the will of God: James 4:2-3

o Not asking in Jesus' name: John 16:24

o Demonic hindrances: Daniel 10:10-13

o Not seeking first, the Kingdom: Only when you seek first the Kingdom are you promised the "other things.": Matthew 6:33

o When you do not know how to pray as you should, prayer is hindered. This is why it is important to let the Holy Spirit pray through you: Romans 8:26

Overcoming The Hindrances:

Remember that identifying hindrances to intercession is not enough, but you must also ask God to help you to eliminate them from your life. Also remember that what seems to be unanswered prayer does not mean there are hindrances in your life. Answers to prayer may be delayed (Luke 18:7) or answered differently from our desires (II Corinthians 12:8-9).

All Intercessors Should:

1. Love God.
2. Love people.
3. Love their pastors.
4. Love their local church.
5. Be pure of heart.
6. Have no hidden agendas or motives.
7. Be righteous and holy.
8. Have a clear conscience.
9. Have no hidden sin.
10. Have no spirit of manipulation or control.
11. Be submitted to Godly authority.

Daily Prayer Times:

This exercise is to help you set daily prayer times. Setting daily times in your phone to pray will help you by ensuring that you stay on schedule. Use this exercise to document your daily prayer times.

I am committing to praying daily at these times:

○ _____

○ _____

○ _____

- _____
- _____
- _____

Daily Prayer Request

During this exercise, document your prayer requests and the very things you are asking God to do for you during your times of prayer.

Today I am being intentional in praying for:

Morning:

- _____
- _____
- _____
- _____
- _____

Afternoon:

- _____
- _____
- _____
- _____
- _____
- _____

Evening:

- ○ _____
- ○ _____
- ○ _____
- ○ _____
- ○ _____
- ○ _____

Morning:

- ○ _____
- ○ _____
- ○ _____
- ○ _____
- ○ _____
- ○ _____

Afternoon:

- ○ _____
- ○ _____
- ○ _____
- ○ _____
- ○ _____
- ○ _____

Evening:

- ○ _____
- ○ _____
- ○ _____
- ○ _____
- ○ _____
- ○ _____

Morning:

- ○ _____
- ○ _____
- ○ _____
- ○ _____
- ○ _____
- ○ _____

Afternoon:

- ○ _____
- ○ _____
- ○ _____
- ○ _____
- ○ _____
- ○ _____

Evening:

○ _____

○ _____

○ _____

○ _____

○ _____

○ _____

Morning:

○ _____

○ _____

○ _____

○ _____

○ _____

○ _____

Afternoon:

○ _____

○ _____

○ _____

○ _____

○ _____

○ _____

Evening:

- ○ _____
- ○ _____
- ○ _____
- ○ _____
- ○ _____
- ○ _____

Morning:

- ○ _____
- ○ _____
- ○ _____
- ○ _____
- ○ _____
- ○ _____

Afternoon:

- ○ _____
- ○ _____
- ○ _____
- ○ _____
- ○ _____
- ○ _____

Evening:

o _____
o _____
o _____
o _____
o _____
o _____

Morning:

o _____
o _____
o _____
o _____
o _____
o _____

Afternoon:

o _____
o _____
o _____
o _____
o _____
o _____

Evening:

O _____

O _____

O _____

O _____

O _____

O _____

Daily Prayer Targets:

This exercise is to help you stay intentional and stay consistent in your seek with God.

Matthew 7:7-8 (TPT) – [7]"Ask, and the gift is yours. Seek, and you'll discover. Knock, and the door will be opened for you. [8]For every persistent one will get what he asks for. Every persistent seeker will discover what he longs for. And everyone who knocks persistently will one day find an open door."

Remember don't stop praying until you see your answers in prayer manifested.

Today I am ASKING God to do:

_____

_____

_____

_____

_____

_____

Today I am Seeking God for:

_____

_____

_____

_____

_____

_____

Today I am believing God for this door to be open:

_____

_____

_____

_____

_____

_____

Today I am ASKING God to do:

_____

_____

_____

_____

_____

Today I am Seeking God for:

_____

_____

_____

_____

_____

Today I am believing God for this door to be open:

_____

_____

_____

_____

_____

Today I am ASKING God to do:

_____

_____

_____

_____

_____

Today I am Seeking God for:

_____

_____

_____

_____

_____

Today I am believing God for this door to be open:

_____

_____

_____

_____

_____

Today I am ASKING God to do:

_____

_____

_____

_____

_____

_____

Today I am Seeking God for:

_____

_____

_____

_____

_____

_____

Today I am believing God for this door to be open:

_____

_____

_____

_____

_____

Today I am ASKING God to do:

_____

_____

_____

_____

_____

_____

Today I am Seeking God for:

_____

_____

_____

_____

_____

Today I am believing God for this door to be open:

_____

_____

_____

_____

_____

Today I am ASKING God to do:

_____

_____

_____

_____

_____

Today I am Seeking God for:

_____

_____

_____

_____

_____

Today I am believing God for this door to be open:

_____

_____

_____

_____

_____

_____

Today I am ASKING God to do:

_____

_____

_____

_____

_____

_____

Today I am Seeking God for:

_____

_____

_____

_____

_____

Today I am believing God for this door to be open:

_____

_____

_____

_____

_____

Today I am ASKING God to do:

_____

_____

_____

_____

_____

Today I am Seeking God for:

_____

_____

_____

_____

_____

_____

Today I am believing God for this door to be open:

_____

_____

_____

_____

_____

Today I am ASKING God to do:

_____

_____

_____

_____

_____

Today I am Seeking God for:

_____

_____

_____

_____

_____

Today I am believing God for this door to be open:

_____

_____

_____

_____

_____

Answered Prayers:

This exercise is designed for you to document your answered prayers.

Daniel 10:12 (NIV) – *"Then he continued, "Do not be afraid, Daniel. Since the first day that you set your mind to gain understanding and to humble yourself before your God, your words were heard, and I have come in response to them."*

Thank you Lord for Answering my prayers:

_____

_____

_____

_____

_____

_____

_____

_____

_____

_____

_____

_____

_____

_____

_____

_____

_____

_____

_____

_____

_____

The Day I Prayed: _____

The Day He answered: _____

Thank you Lord for Answering my prayers:

_____

_____

_____

_____

_____

_____

_____

_____

_____

_____

_____

_____

_____

_____

_____

_____

_____

_____

_____

_____

_____

_____

_____

_____

_____

_____

_____

_____

_____

The Day I Prayed: _____

The Day He answered: _____

Thank you Lord for Answering my prayers:

_____

_____

_____

_____

_____

_____

_____

_____

_____

_____

_____

_____

_____

_____

_____

_____

_____

_____

_____

_____

_____

_____

_____

_____

_____

_____

_____

_____

_____

The Day I Prayed: _____

The Day He answered: _____

Thank you Lord for Answering my prayers:

_____

_____

_____

_____

_____

_____

_____

_____

_____

_____

_____

_____

_____

_____

_____

_____

_____

_____

_____

_____

_____

_____

_____

_____

_____

_____

_____

The Day I Prayed: _____

The Day He answered: _____

Thank you Lord for Answering my prayers:

_____

_____

_____

_____

_____

_____

_____

_____

_____

_____

_____

_____

_____

_____

_____

_____

_____

_____

_____

_____

_____

_____

_____

_____

_____

_____

_____

The Day I Prayed: _____

The Day He answered: _____

Thank you Lord for Answering my prayers:

_____

_____

_____

_____

_____

_____

_____

_____

_____

_____

_____

_____

_____

_____

_____

_____

_____

_____

_____

_____

_____

_____

_____

_____

_____

_____

_____

_____

The Day I Prayed: _____

The Day He answered: _____

Thank you Lord for Answering my prayers:

_____

_____

_____

_____

_____

_____

_____

_____

_____

_____

_____

_____

_____

_____

_____

_____

_____

_____

_____

_____

_____

_____

_____

_____

_____

_____

_____

_____

_____

The Day I Prayed: _____

The Day He answered: _____

Thank you Lord for Answering my prayers:

_____

_____

_____

_____

_____

_____

_____

_____

_____

_____

_____

_____

_____

_____

_____

_____

_____

_____

_____

_____

_____

_____

_____

_____

_____

_____

_____

The Day I Prayed: _____

The Day He answered: _____

Thank you Lord for Answering my prayers:

_____

_____

_____

_____

_____

_____

_____

_____

_____

_____

_____

_____

_____

_____

_____

_____

_____

_____

_____

_____

_____

_____

_____

_____

_____

_____

_____

_____

_____

_____

The Day I Prayed: _____

The Day He answered: _____

Growing in Intercession:

This section is designed for you to document the areas that you would like to grow in prayer.

Challenges in my life of prayer and intercession:

_____

_____

_____

_____

Steps I will take to overcome my challenges:

_____

_____

_____

_____

People that will hold me accountable in my growth:

_____

_____

_____

_____

Challenges in my life of prayer and intercession:

_____

_____

_____

_____

_____

Steps I will take to overcome my challenges:

_____

_____

_____

_____

People that will hold me accountable in my growth:

_____

_____

_____

_____

_____

Challenges in my life of prayer and intercession:

_____

_____

_____

_____

_____

Steps I will take to overcome my challenges:

_____

_____

_____

_____

_____

People that will hold me accountable in my growth:

_____

_____

_____

_____

_____

Challenges in my life of prayer and intercession:

_____

_____

_____

_____

_____

Steps I will take to overcome my challenges:

_____

_____

_____

_____

People that will hold me accountable in my growth:

_____

_____

_____

_____

_____

Challenges in my life of prayer and intercession:

_____

_____

_____

_____

_____

Steps I will take to overcome my challenges:

_____

_____

_____

_____

People that will hold me accountable in my growth:

_____

_____

_____

_____

_____

Challenges in my life of prayer and intercession:

_____

_____

_____

_____

_____

Steps I will take to overcome my challenges:

_____

_____

_____

_____

_____

People that will hold me accountable in my growth:

_____

_____

_____

_____

_____

Challenges in my life of prayer and intercession:

_____

_____

_____

_____

_____

Steps I will take to overcome my challenges:

_____

_____

_____

_____

_____

People that will hold me accountable in my growth:

_____

_____

_____

_____

_____

Challenges in my life of prayer and intercession:

_____

_____

_____

_____

_____

Steps I will take to overcome my challenges:

_____

_____

_____

_____

_____

People that will hold me accountable in my growth:

_____

_____

_____

_____

_____

Challenges in my life of prayer and intercession:

_____

_____

_____

_____

_____

Steps I will take to overcome my challenges:

_____

_____

_____

_____

_____

People that will hold me accountable in my growth:

_____

_____

_____

_____

_____

Challenges in my life of prayer and intercession:

_____

_____

_____

_____

_____

Steps I will take to overcome my challenges:

_____

_____

_____

_____

_____

People that will hold me accountable in my growth:

_____

_____

_____

_____

_____

Measuring My Growth:

This exercise is used to document areas that you have seen growth in your life of prayer:

I have grown in this area of prayer:

_____

_____

_____

_____

_____

_____

_____

I have grown in this area of prayer:

_____

_____

_____

_____

_____

_____

_____

I have grown in this area of prayer:

_____

_____

_____

_____

_____

_____

_____

I have grown in this area of prayer:

_____

_____

_____

_____

_____

_____

_____

I have grown in this area of prayer:

_____

_____

_____

_____

_____

_____

_____

I have grown in this area of prayer:

_____

_____

_____

_____

_____

_____

_____

I have grown in this area of prayer:

_____

_____

_____

_____

_____

_____

_____

I have grown in this area of prayer:

_____

_____

_____

_____

_____

_____

_____

I have grown in this area of prayer:

_____

_____

_____

_____

_____

_____

_____

I have grown in this area of prayer:

_____

_____

_____

_____

_____

_____

_____

Intercessory Keys:

o Whenever God wants to release His plans in the earth, he places it within the womb of an intercessor.

o Intercession causes the Heavens to contract. The prayers of the righteous are the greatest military force on earth.

o Intercessors give God His word back.

o Intercessors are birthers.

o Intercessors push things from the unseen to the seen realm.

Questions:

1. What is an intercessor?

_____

_____

_____

_____

_____

_____

_____

2. Why do you believe you are called to pray?

_____

_____

_____

_____

_____

_____

Intercessors / Intercession:

- Jesus is our example of an intercessor.
- Jesus is interceding and is committed to being an intercessor for us.
- Intercessor – One who has a call to prayer leadership.
- God shares things with intercessors that are not available to other people.
- God shares His secrets with intercessors.

Recognizing Your Call:

o You have consistent pulling to prayer being a solution.
o Intercessors want to respond to things by prayer.
o Intercessors are sensitive people.
o Intercessors pick up on what others need to receive.
o Intercessors are highly burdened people.
o Intercessors, most of the time, always go into prayer for answers.
o Intercessors do most of their work in private.
o Intercessors are awakened.
o Intercessors are driven by justice.
o Intercessors are resilient; they do not easily take no for an answer.
o Intercessors are called by God.
o An intercessor is someone who is all in.
o It takes intercessors a long time to detox from past experiences and traumas.

What is your first response to the presence of God?

Your gift will manifest when the presence of God is in the room.

o Intercessors are hungry for information.
o Intercessors tap into God's ways.
o Intercessors ask God questions.

o Intercessors are a part of Heaven's administration.

There are levels of intercession based on maturity.

o Intercessors talk to God in their minds all day.
o Intercessors must know their release.
o Intercessors are selfless.
o Intercessors must be aware of needs and environment.
o Intercessors are sacrificial people.

Intercessor – Intervener – Interceptor – Interrupter – Inventor

Recognizing Your Grace:

We each have a field in prayer!

Many people have been called to be great intercessors but did not discover their anointing because they were too busy examining the fruit in another person's prayer field. Your field is unique.

Each individual has their own unique identity in prayer and intercession. Never try to mimic or copy another in prayer. Be uniquely you and allow God to be God in you. God has anointed you for a particular purpose. You have different kinds of services but the same Lord. Each one of us has a special prayer mix that we cannot earn, but we can carry to the assignments God has set aside for us to do. There are different functions, but WE HAVE ALL BEEN CALLED TO PRAY!

Different types of graces in intercession:

1. **PRAYER LISTS INTERCESSORS** – Prayer points are written down to be taken before the Lord. People who pray like this are very faithful. Some people get bored praying this way, but some find it rewarding.

2. **GENERAL INTERCESSORS** - Some just like to pray, not limited, or diversified in the way they pray. They love to pray in different ways, not specialized and not restricted in the way they pray. Pray anything and everything.

3. **PERSONAL INTERCESSORS** – Some have been called to pray regularly for a particular individual. These intercessors should pray for wisdom regarding what should be shared.

4. **CRISIS INTERCESSORS** – Some pray for somebody when they have a crisis in their life. These prayers are decisive and at a critical moment. Many times, it can be for a life and death situation. They pray and pray and when it is over, they might never pray for that person again. When God brings someone's face before us it is to pray. Pray that the Holy Spirit makes us sensitive.

5. **INTERCESSORS WHO PRAY FOR THEIR NATION, NATIONS, THEIR CITY, ISLAND, PEOPLE GROUPS** – Some will have a particular interest. Not everyone who prays for their city prays for their country and vice versa.

6. **INTERCESSORS WHO PRAY FOR LEADERS, SPIRITUAL LEADERS, & POLITICAL LEADERS**

7. **INTERCESSORS WHO DON'T PRAY FOR ANYTHING POLITICAL BUT FOR A CHURCH OR MINISTRY WHERE THEY ARE INVOLVED.**

8. **INTERCESSORS WHO PRAY FOR THEIR FAMILIES** – Often true with women as they have a special desire for their families.

9. **MERCY INTERCESSORS** – Those who pray for those that need healing for people who are hurt- both emotionally and physically. These intercessors might read the newspaper and cry out for those who are hurting, people who walk the hospitals.

10. **FINANCIAL INTERCESSORS** – They pray for a release of finances so that the gospel will reach the world and for special projects, etc.

11. **INTERCESSORS WHO PRAY FOR SOULS** – Ultimately, this is for the purpose of evangelism.

12. **WARFARE INTERCESSORS** – They are always fighting the enemy in prayer.
    o These intercessors need some preparation to go to war in prayer victoriously.
    o The will to win.
    o "Have knowledge of the enemy. The greater the knowledge of the enemy the

greater the victory."

- o Have an adequate source of supply – What is our supply? Research and timing.
- o Some who are warring never spend any time at the feet of Jesus. This should be our most important goal --to cling to Him and to have an intimate relationship with Him.
- o Jesus didn't do anything He didn't see His Father do. *DON'T PULL DOWN STRONGHOLDS IF YOU DON'T KNOW WHAT YOU ARE DOING.*

13.   **RESEARCH INTERCESSORS** - Love to do research. They thrive on prayerfully collecting facts about strongholds and principalities.

Remember: WE MUST KNOW OUR PLACE AND TO BE READY WHEN GOD CALLS. Realize that we are fighting against principalities and powers - not PEOPLE. We need to try to see the spirit that is behind the actions. Too many people are hurt in the body of Christ warfare waged against people instead of against principalities and powers.

14. WORSHIP INTERCESSORS - They usually worship from the prospect of victory. An example is

Miriam with the tambourine. These intercessors may use instruments, dance, kneeling, bowing or any other act of worship in intercession.

15. PROPHETIC INTERCESSOR – These are intercessors who are assigned to discern what Heaven is preparing to release in the earth realm and to birth the will, purpose, and plan of God in the earth realm through travail and consistent communication with God.

o Prophetic intercessors carry the burden of the Lord and only pray wat they hear Heaven speaking.

16. THE WATCHMAN INTERCESSOR – Build prayer hedges, guard, and protect individuals, nations, assignments, teams, regions, and nations.

17. PRIESTLY INTERCESSOR – One who pleads the cases of others before the throne room of Heaven in prayer. Heb. 4:16

18. PRAYER WARRIOR – Intercessors who are assigned to receive and implement warfare strategies to overthrow powers of darkness and release breakthrough. These intercessors have a militant spirit and are skilled in the art of warfare. Ephesians 6:12, Ephesians 6:18, Matthew 11:12.

o Intercessors are the military strategists of the body of Christ and Kingdom of God. Prayer warriors unleash Jehovah Gibbor.
o Prayer warriors receive downloads and instructions on how to win and combat demonic forces.
o Prayer warriors are fighters.
o Prayer warriors breakthrough in prayer.

We are all different, and God anoints us differently. Find your anointing and be set free to move with it. Don't be exclusive, you may move in more than one way. God has anointed you for this hour of prayer.

Now that you have read some of the different graces in intercession, what is your grace? What area of intercession are you called to? Remember you can be called to more than one area of intercession.

1. What is your grace (s)?

_____

_____

_____

_____

_____

_____

_____

_____

2. What area of Intercession are you called to?

_____

_____

_____

_____

_____

_____

_____

_____

_____

Declare this: *"I am committing to my place of prayer and Intercession and no matter what obstacles or challenges come my way I will remain committed to my life of prayer and Intercession."*

Made in the USA
Columbia, SC
20 February 2025

54116924R00078